For Gilly,

with love,

Walter Saunders

April, '76. (cruellest
month etc.)

BATELEUR
PRESS
JOHANNESBURG
1975

Bateleur Poets

ABRAHAMS
GREIG
KIRKWOOD
SAUNDERS

First published 1975 by *Bateleur Press*
4 Pallinghurst Road
Parktown, Johannesburg

Distributed by C. Struik (Pty) Ltd, P.O. Box 1144, Cape Town

ISBN 0 620 01807 0

Designed by Wim Reinders
Printed by Creda Press (Pty) Ltd, 19 Bree Street, Cape Town
Bound by Edward D. Seabrook, 19 Bree Street, Cape Town

The motifs on the cover, fly-leaf and
title page are spirit figures from rock shelters
in the Natal Drakensberg

CONTENTS

BATELEUR POETS

The aim of this series, Bateleur Poets, is to publish what is excellent
in South African verse today. We want the books we publish
to show off the verse to best advantage but we also want them to be as
reasonably priced as today's printing costs will allow. By bringing out
these four poets in one volume the cost per book has been reduced
while the quality of printing and paper has not suffered. However,
the intention of this experiment is to give each poet exactly the same
space as he would have had in a separate book; thus each section has
its own title and list of contents. There are four poets here,
but beyond this material fact no further unity has been intended.
It is hoped that readers and reviewers will come to each poet as a
fresh experience, that they will respect the integrity of each section.

No unity was intended but it is a fact that the poets in this volume
are all white, English speaking and South African. But that is the end
of it. We will publish anything that we think is good, by anyone of this
country. Certainly the verse in this volume differs widely in content
and expression. Perhaps the only unifying link is a concern for the
language the poets use, how it is to be changed, directed and shaped
to this ambience: a brutal and subtle challenge.
A concern for language is a concern for excellence. That, we hope,
is what this series is about.

Patrick Cullinan

Thresholds of Tolerance

LIONEL ABRAHAMS

Lionel Abrahams, born 1928 in Johannesburg, was
educated at the Hope Home, Damelin College and Wits;
introduced to literature by H. C. Bosman and became
editor of his posthumous volumes; edited
The Purple Renoster; co-edited, with Nadine Gordimer,
S.A. Writing Today (Penguin Books) as a demonstration
against the 'gagging clause'; founded Renoster Books
which published the first books by Oswald Mtshali,
Wally Serote, Eva Royston and Robert Royston.

CONTENTS

Several of these poems have been published before, in
New Coin, Contrast, Ophir, The Purple Renoster and *New S.A. Writing* (PEN).
To the editors and publishers concerned due acknowledgement is hereby made.

WITH WEATHER

A thousand streets of my home my native city
I have never seen,
and today the familiar roads look strange.

Today soft clouds unevenly cover the sky
after those warm blue lucky weeks
and a breeze ruffles town with rumours of altering season
and brief puffs of steamy rain.

My heart is somehow naked,
outside me on a jerking thread:
unaccumstomedly exposed, it is chilled by this tender weather.

Yet only tomorrow will spring retire,
making way for the due remainder of winter.

The old routes have a new look,
reflection of my impatience:
I have been these ways once too often.

A tree in the weather rides tomorrow
like a pale green kite,
at a corner I never turned before.

CONTACT

Coming with kumquats
(my dinner-guest's offering in a paper bag)
I crossed sixteen streets of Hillbrow traffic,
and the last the worst, like a crocodile stream –
which swum in seven choked seconds,
I bogged on its bank,
my stepping foot nerve-stuck on the high kerb.
Reed-rooted over the gutter, I tottered,
headlit in the car-swished eddies, sweating.
Right moment . . .
a gate swung and a backyard boozer rhinoed out
looking to horn me mid-stream,
zagged off my danger,
just . . .

but drew after him, hurling screams like assegais,
a huntress.
"Baas," she wailed to my whiteness,
"call the police he wants to kill my husband."
I called God and succumbed to the sidewalk,
spilling some forty red-gold testicles.

MACHINES TAKING OVER

    Down there Excavator
nudged and nibbled and chawed
at the red earth,
pawed and nibbled and scooped up bellyfuls.
    Shyly, coyly, pretending no interest,
Truck tippytoed down the screwshaped ramp,
moaning with the delicacy, the importance of it all;
braked dead at every dangerous corner,
then, lurching and humping with desire, came on,
came back end, receptive end, on –
pretending no connection
but flashing question and seduction
from the sly corner of a twisted eye.
    The laden shovel dangled
till eye met eye, then in stages,
one pulse-worth at a time,
Excavator's great part jerked straight
and swivelled up, up.
Truck, hip by finicky hip, sidled in close,
now shuddered just below,
now rocked with joy at the coming,
the thunderous opening that loaded her belly.

PROFESSIONAL SECRET

    The voice between fashion notes and the serial
did not dispel the tea-time calm of Woman's Hour:
distinguished visitor, senior international nurse,
kindly recalling episodes from an interesting career.
". . . Arriving while the guns could still be heard,
our first job in the Camp

was to sort out those we could save"
– the rest about the rest she left unsaid.
"Next came delousing:
we wore overalls, turbans, gloves,
trousers tucked into high boots,
worked on marble slabs
applying hard brushes all over the naked skins
– some like paper, but several surprising cases survived.
The lice once gone, the typhus death rate fell
to only twenty a day,
and within five weeks none from that cause.
We ran the whole Camp, of course, as a hospital:
those who weren't ill were in a bad way from starvation.
We had to feed them all on milk and honey
or they'd have died . . ."
        This expert on aftermaths,
mileposting her life with disasters,
was undistracted by distinctions one might draw
between the natural and the calculated cataclysm:
Skopje as much her job as Nagasaki.
She trailed death's binges with a minimum of disgust
(". . Still miles away we began to smell the stench . .")
to clean-up-after, make all possible repairs,
bringing to the business her special indifferent vigour
and no questions about Causes.
The smokestacked signs of automated rage
stirred no answering rage for her to tremble with;
for routines of hate she presumed no compensatory
paralysing love;
tenderness would have chained her useful hands,
prevented Red Cross holy work.
        I wonder if intended listeners inferred
the same brute hint that stalks me through her story:
The theoried overmen
who cater death's gross feasts, do more
– infect the whole race so
our hands must be as hard as those that kill,
and scrubbed clean of the carrier, passion,
to bring the living milk and honey.

BIRDS ABOUT JOHANNESBURG

Georges Braque in his final mystic years
dwelt on the joy and awfulness of birds.
Prophecy at the last loses its personal point,
yet he at eighty drew off for his friends
portentous lithographs of living flight.
One rare set now reaching this far town
for intimate display and sale
releases to our street-ruled eyes
a heightened sense of moving wings
seen or remembered,
renews and magnifies
the meaning visibility of birds.

Leaving the city we again found
the half forgotten self of the city
that earlier day of this mild winter.
Under stripped sky a scraped down dump
outtopping some warehouse or factory block
redolent of labour and demolition
huddled over the exit route:
these gave it to us, a final bony shape
pecked clean as though by a vulturous sun –
the city pure, as it knew itself young
and now growing new still has to know.

Treeless, tawny with silver grass,
outside, the tableland moved us with mystery
hiding nothing but time
and birds in the folds of distance.
Long wings that rowed on a low lake of air
kept level and abreast of our skimming eyes;
dip-darting in a blur of brown seedheads
that bird seemed fixed, just bobbing at anchor
until, outsped, it swam into our wake.
Innocent as Eden the birdwide highveld
knew what it knew.

The night that a brief colder spell began
a restless black wind brooded over the house.
Its chill plumes dangled down from the sky,
covered the city,
suffocated the shivering veld.

While I tried to sleep
an indifferent rapacious bird
was devouring the stars.

The city, insistent, knows its own newness.
Square into virgin depths of the birdspace
new shafts corridor daily upward,
mocking Tiresias with windows
that have seen nothing but know all.
The trellised cranes they elevate
seem stiff-winged giant birds
which sidle, wheel and dominate
but, skeletons already, can foretell
only their own contracted fall –
or unstill crucifixes raised to bear
our burdens of knowing and agitation.

The three storeyed place where the painter
hired a modest studio
among watchmakers, milliners, machinists
and two fortune-tellers at least,
is collapsing in noises, fragments and dust.
Its tenants have gone their separated ways.
Its doorway no longer invites the leap
of those sculpted buck at the opposite fountain.
Off the grass in the fountain garden,
shallow niche of retreat from the street,
people cloaked with the shadows of people,
whites on the benches, blacks on the ledges,
waiting watch one near crane's motion,
the demolition, passers-by,
the frozen buck over the leaping water,
and the bleached lawn where a hundred dark pigeons
graze and shimmer.
(Soon some sharp report or roar
may spurt them into shattered air
to stir and fan and prophesy.)

Naked the sky is offering
the soft lovemaking of the sun.
The stroked city lies tense between stiff shadows,
grows implacable, knows what it knows,
always a whisper of menace,
the patient wheel of metallic vultures.

Hovering lower than skyscrapers
the frostwhite afternoon moon
is revealed in the suburb,
threequarters full, enormous parachute
but in ascent
lifting beyond our reach and our knowing
some burden of rescue or threat.
Below, as I watch and grope,
shadows of two pigeons streak the banked grass verge.
I look for these unawed familiars. There.
Tenebrous now, now flickering the light,
weaving swift lattices of flight-and-chase-and-flight,
they whir and circle vast in the brittle air.

WALK

Hands aweave in a tiny slow-fin-motion,
see-saw float of her daintily balanced butt,
skirt-pleats' neat little lapped reed lilt
all imply a brimful cup, lake or ocean
that she bears and from which dares not
let one drop be spilt.

SOWETO FUNERAL

("Familiarity is the kingdom of the lost"
– *Dugmore Boetie*, died November, 1966)

Behind us the horizon's tide
has drowned the known Johannesburg.
A man we thought we knew
has brought us to a place he never meant.
The road veers, tacks,
entangling us like tourists in uncompassed afternoon.
Mine dumps, the outpost power station,
and even, miles ago, the lighthouse tip
of the strategic tower
have sunk away:
now nothing dares to interrupt the sky

or curtail distances –
yet still this dormitory world of low new huts
in ranked batallions, uniform by blocks,
quilts the tilting hugeness of the veld.

House patterns A, B, C, D, E
in turn insist their order to our eyes;
among children and churchgoers
green commonage wheels by and rears
a stallion up to mount a tall white mare;
a cortege for another cemetery
crosses our curiosity
mourning another dead with the pale fierce glare
of headlamps lit as though grief snuffs the sun.

But the road has business for us:
angling across the ruled townships
the road is a graph
through scattered sheets of tabulations;
the road is tracking down
the block we can't avoid.

The cemetery finds us.
We weave its smaller maze until
among ranged mounds the hacked hole calls.
Joined to a burial gathering,
languageless, we stand without its hymns,
pinned to a faceless coffin on a metal rail.
The towering sun could be our landmark
but beneath this naked sky
the flare of what we think we know
burns low: one name
seems all that we can recognise.
We throw clods on the fact we came to con.
Other mourners pile earth and wreaths
and cancel out our license to be here
with thanks that we have come; these name us
aliens from the tall white town
which hardly feels this second city
plunging on its haunch.

I began today
unwishingly intent
to reach one Sunday suburb more

of mortal knowledge –
yet hardly hold the thought of this man's death,
and stray instead the nameless ravelled streets
of my live ignorance.
The lodgers of these rigid rows
who know the way in their stark
neighbour kingdom
may have a meaning when *they* say
familiarity.

MAXIMS OF GODHEAD AND MANHOOD

Was Adam mud or breath of God
before God breathed and made the man?
Decide, decide!
– The question's void.

Poems intone the poets who seem to sing.
Bricks build their architects.
The pigments crucify
that painter who invokes epiphany.

Gut is the root,
God is the fruit,
I am the tree.

Earth out of earth, I extend
through element and tissue,
organ, function, faculty.

My foulness feeds the living earth,
my dreams have built elysium.

Visions and lusts are of one holy piece
and lust can be Godly lustre:
whatever is Aware
gives birth to God.

Divide me from divine is deicide.

The stench from Adam's stirring mud
was the first breath of God.

OCTOBER TWILIGHT

Sunken the sun is releasing from day
long rivers of sky that run
with swirls and whirpools of swallows –
quick carbon flakes swooping the roofs,
star-small where the eye
dives to the depths of the cool height,
and smaller
because the exploding living air
is deeper.

POETRY: TWO REMARKS

I
All I can show of words
or say of worlds or wars,
love, virtue, godhead,
all my truths
are pawnmoves in some intellectual chess.
My childhood's first impress
of milkblue lakewaves
through black clustered trees
was philosophical
beyond the range of speech.

II
(For R.M.)

Ruth in this tree.
Scoured stones, wrung brine
and something broken at the root –
thin as this thorny air
its whiplash branches spare us
our due scoring,
yield us shade for shelter,
tongue-rejoicing fruit.

CITIZEN DICE

("The straight sidewalks of Eloff Street
were never made for human feet."
– *Herman Charles Bosman*)

Something is taking this gamble,
spinning the roulette-months
(what day will we fall on,
odd or black or . . . . ?)
rattling the cup
of the fleshy foreign element.

From these dice expect only the unexpected.

    O city, o container,
    scour out this excess,
    simplify, hollow your space,
    your logical coming perfection
    of emptiness.

Pressed into place
on the ruled walk of the paving squares
we meet eye to eye
the timed wink of the robot,
our face rationalised,
our head callipered,
cancelled our self-willed eyes
with shining blinds
that miniature the blocked skyline –
below, our mouth
is wild with appetite.

In the box of the bus a girl
devouring apricots
has seemed to eat herself.

    Machine-city
    utilise me, stuff of your processes
    integrate me, part of your parts.
    Convent-city, convert me
    exact my vows,
    my chastity, my poverty,
    my conformity.

City, subdue my unrest,
quell me.

A swelling oyster, can we overfill
the city's ridged and fastened shell?

Some reward for one or two senses:
piled fruit, petals still unfolding
and refolding
clash the greying thickened air.
Are we the battle square of flowers
whose cut stems clash on granolithic troughs,
barricades of pyramided fruits?

The doorway women desiccate
waiting for what they must await,
this to count up, that to forget.

City, we spill,
contain us,
we wander, sort us
shuttle us in and between
your straight shafts and categories.
Illuminate us:
in the pubis of your shadows, unrooted
we swell with our heats
and we bloom.

Up certain streets I stare
with hectic license of the roving eye.

On certain streets I've heard a working song,
endless weave of a tribal refrain:
a burst of shrapnel became birds again.
Gutter sweeper, sing sweetly
till my bus has come.
Pressed into place
we overflow and burst splash blood
in basins and gutters semen
on the cement floor
graffiti on the varnished door.
In the neither forbidding
nor permitting
rationed intimacy of the bus

some secretly unsheathed knife-thigh
rapes or is raped by
my furtive eyes
as vulnerable as grapes.

Where is the place for tenderness?
Our noisome softness is incongruous.

Some reward for one or two senses:
my teeth will lance the soft white of this pear.
Girl, give me your hand to hold,
hear my secret out –
I'm not yet mechanised or dead
and alien still the gutter sweeper sings.

    City, my garden,
    root me.
    Woman city, open
    your rectilinear hollows,
    admit me to your orderly embrace,
    press me into place.

Our softness is incongruous.
Our cut stems rot.
Something gets ready to topple us
out of the stupendous iron
dicing cup of the city.

THRESHOLDS OF TOLERANCE

In this climate of storms
the streets shine with tears.
Let those who have eyes
let those who have anger
set strong faces toward the streets.

I turn inside my room
turn, turn.
If I have strength
if I am blessed with vision
I shall possess my private life.

That poet's naked nerves
thunder:
there are days when even beauty
appals him,
he turns his paintings to the walls.

But I, inside my room
I can't be frightened.
I choose nightmare drawings
and paintings that are full of grief.
Behind my door, in the quiet,
I hunt my private life.

YOGA

One is not the body:
revelation of his third hour
in the lotus position since dawn.
One is not the mind:
lesson of the undirection of thought.
Behind the sternum Atman glows.
One knows One is.

I rise late, eat sweet slops,
visit the trading city, shop
for my own face, my memorable name,
trade words for words, haggle
for love in my flesh, grapple
to know what's known.
A hollow of breath behind the bone.
I am not my body.
I am not my mind.
I never sought this knowledge.

FOR CHARLES EGLINGTON

A land without ruins
is not where you easily learn that to fall
or be felled is the only condition of victory.
The truimph that survives the fighting,

flaunts and takes the spoils
is easy purchase, Pick & Pay,
and stoics, assured their aspect of virtue endures,
scholars who have caught a corner of the scheme
and can explain (or explain why there's to be
no explanation), saints, heroes, stars
are neon flash.
The maths-man or the mystic in the void
or the clown juggling apples, punning on the news
to no one, down in chaos
breathes Buddha breath.
Fall singing, die and laugh,
praise the gone gods,
philosophize when you have understood
that none's meaning stands.
While your contracted decades wrinkle to the lines
of the only binding clauses, blindly be.
Not because life is One
or truth accumulates
like the cells of a foetus.
Going on is because the habits do this,
the hormones do that.
Poet's lines, thus, are star courses and climates,
and the poet's suicide is death by natural causes.

LITERATURE

Their tongues burst open,
their heads explode and their eyes,
all their organs of sense and sensation.
The earth is exploding,
the sky is exploding.
They go inside the explosions
with their exploding words.

I polish my glasses, my face,
photographs of old streets,
of the deceased and of the beloved.
Look! I'm expecting to say,
Look! This is how it is.

THE WHITEMAN BLUES

Two cars, three loos, a swimming pool,
Investment paintings, kids at a private school . . .
we entertain with shows or gourmet food –
and yet we don't feel right, we don't feel good.

Why doesn't the having help?
Why doesn't the spending save?
Why doesn't the fun –
Why doesn't the culture –
Why don't the ads add up to something?

We can afford to say we know
the blacks are really given hell,
Big Boss is harsh and stupid and must go:
we say it – and it helps like one Aspro.
We still feel jumpy, mixed up, not quite well.

Which specialist can cure the thing we've got –
the got-it, gotta-get-it blues,
the deep-freeze, cheaper wholesale, world excursion blues?
We're high on the know-all-about-it booze.
We're bursting with kwashiokor of the bank.
We're depressed by the whiteman blues.

In the backyards they pray for us.
In Soweto they see our plight.
in the border areas they understand.
In the Bantustans they wait
to pat our shoulder, hold our hand.
They know, they know,
to them it isn't news:
we've got these lost-man, late-man,
money-man, superman,
whiteman blues.

LAMENT

On the death of my mother, Anna Abrahams, née
Lieberman, born Vilna, 1st March 1900, died
Johannesburg, 1st February 1970.

("Sh'mai Yisroel . . ." – first words of the ritual
affirmation: "Hear, o Israel, the Lord our God,
the Lord is one."

"Extolled and hallowed be the name of the Lord
through all the world . . ." – first words of the
mourner's prayer, "Kaddish".)

There is ending.
as there is beginning.
Were there no beginning there would be no end.
Logic betrays us.
In the beginning was the word,
the whorl, the whore, the hole.
Sh'mai Israel! Hear, o nations, hear!
Thy god, the word without image, is one,
and his name begins with D.
His first commandment was "Ignore!"
And he commanded us again
against the taking of his name.
Yet, nations, hear!
This lord, this one word which is all
moved at the first and made the world,
in his imagelessness made heaven and earth
one squared-off hole.

The pyramids point it,
thrusting mind-sloped angles up
to fill god's hole.
And slaves were we to Pharaoh,
pimps, flattering his denying lust,
raising his stony wedge erect
for god's lascivious hole –
when we and suffocated concubines,
the sphinx and Egypt's dust
begot a swaddled immortality,
gag of logic and the hole.
   God's-man Moses brought us out,
lead-tongued conductor of dying,
purged us by decades and drought
and taught us a subtler piety:
Ignore and praise! Ignore and praise the hole –
that is the law.

24

(I've known orgasm in a public bus
because my law-reigned eyes made free
in some uncaring girl's skirt-shadowed privacy –
thighs wedging to a final white
triangle of cloth
veiling nothing, beginning, hole,
furred maw of any city block.)
Squared-off cold entrances, our common temple portals
make it straight with god,
lay him, pack him tight in 90-angle lines
to bear inane dimensions when he's ripe.
You nations, see, the lord thy god the box,
the lord is one. His first commandment was,
"Knowledge, growing on this tree – ignore."

"The first big thing has happened to you,"
my sister said, placing in my life
our mother struggling into death beneath our eyes.
Mere minutes – how do I count such time? –
from serving Sunday tea and searching out
a makeshift curtain for her daughter's flat,
to the tooth-edged yellow stillness of the mouth
in the blue head: she'd hated waste
and wasted no time dying. Struggling
and not taking on that "look of peace"
she used to tell us that the dead take on:
she'd seen it in her mother's, in her sister's face.
Their deaths were slow: perhaps
her look of peace came on after
the men in berets, the oxygen mask,
the stretcher and muffled ambulance doors
had claimed her from us.
To me she showed no meaning look. I only saw
her turn into a thing, thrust before she guessed
her transmutation had begun.

"The first big thing . . ."
I'd shrunk it in my mind, to one among the certainties
I coolly counted when the decade turned:
by 1980 she would not be alive –
frail, pale, galvanic to our wants,
she was burning out; strange thought, but one
that had its place and size;
death, a process I would process,

was one fact of life.
It would "happen" to her, not to me –
to my daily-seen mother who,
we now begin to see, view blurring view,
was not so easily seen.

    Rooted in her earth, I scarcely saw
some fineness lined in her parchment face
which made so many of my friends,
first meeting her, declare their wonder.
I saw, beyond the hands that "did" for me,
a mainly good puritanical woman,
dutiful, nervous, given to recalcitrant debate
in which her tiredness or my logic
would betray me.

She believed, like her father and brothers,
in Russia, progress, the future,
cancellation of nations, of churches, of money,
and a benign faceless fate
to guard and see man right.
A servant all her years
who hardly knew getting or spending,
she hoarded fancy goods and trash
she was proud to turn, with clever hands,
to thrifty use for us she counted hers.
She wore no graces, served no greeds, pretences,
bore impatiently with her servants,
dealt at times abrasively with those she had to serve,
faced defensively invaders of her house –
the stranger who might prove a fool or sponge or trickster,
the flies she swatted, ants she crushed
or drowned without compunction.
Her mercies had their known unwasteful direction:
I watched her face writhe once
when I, just fallen, writhed for breath,
and saw my hurt happening to her –
who every time I stumbled tore
some nerve-taut fibre in her heart.

But now, o my hubris!
this, in the earth to my root,
this has happened to me.
I know nothing. Death takes us, and nothing.

Life is one light fact of the facts of death.
She who bore me
bore this for me.
I can name the names of my dead,
have named some through years
and the portion of dying I did or escaped
when they died – I can number and name,
and the names that the latest year took were enough,
counting youth and friendship and guilt and art,
to bloat the mind with Death, and the heart.
Yet my eyes had known nothing, my fingers, my ears,
the lungs I now wept with and the bowels of my terror
had known nothing, nothing of death
    (a deaf adolescent learns eggs are laid by hens;
    a Belsen survivor laughs at his first sight
    of a personal funeral)
nothing, nothing before
my mother on the floor
turned blue to her ears and drowned for breath
bearing for me the common stranger
Death.

Grief's quick root green in my brain,
I know the certain medicine:
forget, or madden till you die.
Neglect forgetting and the mind
grows dropsical remembering
to remember who recalls
that someone loved or marked of note
or needed much
once lived, then died.

Two days from hers came Bertrand Russell's death.
Their other points of approach:
each face was spare of flesh, each head was white,
each disbelieved in God and war,
and, as her brothers had,
with Tolstoy and Shaw,
she honoured him.
Her monument: our plausible family memory.
The treasury of rags, wires, shards she stacked
and raked to conjure substitutes
for things else to be bought,
was riddled, rid and ravaged in a week.

Her craft was caring; she bore no caring-for
and died of self-neglect.
We have some photos of her – not at work.
   Earl Russell, as the saying goes, will live –
courageous, clear, his contributions
to the modes of thought will ease
tomorrow's calculations, straighten out
tomorrow's intricate debate.
   Does logical Lord Russell anywhere explain
my error which divines his labours vain?
I see only vortex of time:
remembers of his rememberers will be
remembered by survivors
charged with unreasoned faith
by something in the genes.
In civilization's passing plate
he dropped a coin or two
for entropy to take.

Humanness is a habit.
Yesterday, today and tomorrow
print consequences into someone's genes.
The most adaptable of animals
outlives defeat of Baal and loss of Babylon,
cancellation of a dozen scripts,
the disappointment of alchemy,
survives the poles, the seabeds, Everest,
the cosmic vacuum, orbits to the moon,
and churches that decree demise
of Pancreative Deity.
The furless biped with his tongues and tools
adjusts to what he can't survive –
one poison that he drinks alone.
Lemmings and elephants which have a place of death
submit like a vomiting child
or a man unselved by madness, nightmare, drug –
now is now . . .
But only man can know both that man is
and that he dies.
His survivors and their survivors
to some ultimate generation,
with quenched stars, enter entropy,
verily, they die.

So what is the wisdom of follies?
What is the evil of good?
Let us all be kings
and fall to our knees and eat grass.
Grass passeth but knows not it dies.
Its green moment is forever.
The cricket whose bell
I synchronise with the ticking of a clock
chirps forever.
Only we build clocks and wind them.
Only we carve dates on stones
and make them solemn and watch them topple,
we dupes of tomorrow.
   Our saving tomorrows
matter according to genetic cause.
The shield of David is in the genes.
The crucifixion is in the genes.
The crescent moon is in the genes.
Nirvanah is in the genes.
The hammer-and-sickle is in the genes.
Pigmentation is a cause in the genes.
The humanist tradition is received in the genes.
Say we're programmed to believe.
   I believe in Art the father,
   Maths the mother,
   Cash the holy ghost.
   Philosophy is my consolation.
   Thy bat and thy ball they comfort me
   in the presence of opposing teams.
   The flicks will disport me.
   And Everysister sex will go with me
   and be my guide where e'er the nights I dream,
   in my most need, perhaps, be at my side.

Believing, some make gardens – one I know
with herb beds, moonflowers, liquidamber,
a vista to pastel water, and the birds.
Birds must
know note follows note
and fish feel cause and consequence –
though root and rock submit
to process, stasis or reverse
numb, indifferent if the way
is back to fire or dust

or hurling into entropy, or God.
Can the mindless cosmos say "before" or "after"
to define the moment of a falling leaf?
Would it be falling, hanging,
rising to the branch?
Without cognition, earth as well whirls west
or out of spring to winter
or stirs no way at all,
as steers through day and year.
Time is a warp that's woven onto mind.
    The cosmic hypodermic, man
injecting mind among the molecules,
absent-minded earns an epitaph.
Forgetting the forgetting that will get
the last swirl of the final reading breath,
he grows Mankind and saintly,
finds God and cause and self
and ages and their monuments.
Museums of antique cash and trash,
potsherds and bones we came from
seem to prove we're going somewhere
of concern: an end worth warring for.

Christ on the cross marked a crisis.
But the choosing is always a lie.
Christ on the cross, forsaken by his Silence
filled that hiatus up
with gall and agony and faith.
The nations' one god is an empty cave.
His name begins with D.
His great commandment was
taste gall and agony and faith
and never name my name for that is vain.
His first commandment was,
"Eat thou the sweetness and Ignore!"

Time makes death, but we make time.
I have time to try to know our time,
time to make a poem known.
You have time for your scholarly tome,
and you for a garden with birds.
We have time to ask each other for a light
to soothe the nerves
or show the path

or mitigate the fright;
we have time to set the mouth against the mouth,
the pumping hand against the failing rib,
time to hold back the spinning life
in the vortex whose meaning winds
and unwinds time.
   Hoarders of the trash of time,
we find time to make tomorrow.
We find time to take the six year medical course,
and a percentage of students will fall down cliffs on vacation.
We find time for the depth analysis,
and time for the endowment policy to mature.
We have time to make decades of war;
time to delay the peace conference
at the wrongly shaped table;
time in the condemned cell
to postpone the law with petitions,
and time, while we die, to shorten the time
of one we think we have sentenced to die.
We know of time the things we will not know.
The warder who "burned" the conspirator
will lie on boards while ants devour his balls,
and will not know it.
The spy will have his intimate relics
sorted through by strangers,
and will not know it.
The public executioner will have his day
without advance notice of the time.
The leader will fall,
his successor will succeed to death;
the victor and the vanquished will die
and the difference between them at last
will be unremembered by those of that time.

This is the time when there is no time.
This is the time that death made.
Death we had made of the time we had made.
Time is without us – there is no time,
none,
none to abide the folly it tutors,
      the wounds it heals,
      the tide-bound men it never waits for –
      the doctors, the heroes, the answering sages!

None to await the passing of my evil
        assured that inaction will leave me safe;
none to abide the bringing of my desire
        assured that my actions will spare me alive.
No time to prove the seed of this time,
        since the seed of destruction time will destroy.
        and the fruit of the good seed time will destroy.
There is no time for all the law,
since some of the laws devour the time of some –
though the Law for all is one
whether obeying all
or breaking those laws that break.

Logic betrays us but we do what we can.
"How well you manage!" the kind sometimes exclaim.
She, too, when I forestalled her ever-ready hand,
applauded my slice of cake or glass of milk:
"The things you can do yourself!"
Her light laurels turned my head, against my head.
None do more than power and need allow,
And who would choose less? We do what we can.
   She was tired, hungry for time
to stretch in the sun, or sit
at her increasingly secret piano
I twice overheard in her last five years,
or rest with a radio talk or a page of jokes
or a slowly traversed book, or sleep
her readily broken sleep. Tired,
yet quick-moving – approaching her span
she moved like one in her forties –
urgent with all "the things that have to be done":
The meal to cook, the fruit to pick,
so-and-so's dress to widen or hem,
the socks to do, a wall to wash, pyjamas to patch,
a grandchild's appetite to restore;
our comforts to bring, our day-dreams to water down,
our troubles or triumphs to well up for.
She did what she could. We do what we can.

Doing, there is no time to enquire
why I hate what I hate,
Time only for anger, the angry act.
there is no time to learn
the whence or the where of my possible love –

time only to work (not labour to canalise
or justify the days, but to fill their streambed
with movement from the twisting course
of breath, lymph, semen, blood),
time only to help and be helped,
to receive and to give,
and to give even time.

Sh'mai, Israel, hear!
Ignore, ignore!
There leaks into galactic space
by time's lit fissure
man's lord, thy one god, one.
Do not speak the D name, damned name, Death name.
We speak it with breath and time
while we die.
Let us rather raise him from the dead!
O men of the nations, sh'mai . . .
One coming god,
his name is
I.

Talking Bull

ROBERT GREIG

"After being born in Johannesburg in 1948, I was schooled at Pridwin, then banished to the barbarian wilds of Natal to a WASP factory called Michaelhouse. The less said about that, the better. From there, I went to the University of the Witwatersrand to read English, Political Science and History. I also learnt about anti-apartheid protest and student politics, but my years at Wits were academically (in the narrow sense) undistinguished.

I emigrated to Cape Town, tried working as an advertising copywriter and finally settled into reporting for The Cape Times. This led to reviewing poetry, writing feature articles and being a ballet critic. However, the curse of ambition got me back to Johannesburg as arts editor of a right wing magazine which I escaped for a job as theatre and cinema critic on The Star."

CONTENTS

Acknowledgements are due to: *Bolt, Izwi, New Coin,*
Contrast, Ophir, New, Nation, Detroit News, Leeu-Gamka Dagblad.

TALKING BULL

The engines gulp the air as we heel,
not over that squat, rumpled mountain
and the generous laugh of the bay –
that is for tourists, first arrivals –
but over the tawny flats, acned
with salt-bush. Here and there below
something blinding white and waving
snags the eye. It's no farewell,
but sheets out to bleach the way
skin cannot, or is it (shrinking now)
a shack, trying to keep its cool
in light?

I turn away from that sight never lost
but face my neighbour, all set to talk
of rugby, shares and general elections.
Rather that bleak hide below
of a tied-down bull, bucking the plane
with hot exhalations, mounding how far
into distance I do not know.
Nor how many times my steel cocoon
has cut the air, each time
cooping all space and earth
into portholes less than a head.

That would be good to believe;
and a life spent watching shapes
through speedy windows, or taking
this meat and wine of right.
But I know the gulf of nothing below
that waits, makes me hesitate,
savouring speed. The landings are easy
to handle, even exciting (my neighbour's queasy)
and the way sight accepts a clutter of clouds
and eager, follows the plane's bat-shadow
that slicks across ground, is scooped
flat beneath the still wheels now.

Greeting one's own shadow is harder:
it can't home in the whites-only door.
We cannot go on this way, always parting,
always up in the air, except

telling travellers' tales of savage distance.
So soon forgotten, become abstract, so soon
not knowing how to describe the here to there
or this to that.

DRINKING CAPE REDS

Few refuse good wine. It's part
of the good life. Some there are
who call ours foul, go to pains
to sip the French on their stoeps,
other stick right by white.

But there's more than wine in a bottle:
the old houses, backed by mauve mountains,
their heads in cumulus gables
that gaze on green corps of vines,
in postcards, on labels.

The estate is best reached at sundown
when, gold as the rings of the slavebell,
light vanishes among vineleaves
and all is waxy as yellowwood.
The slaves are departed, save those

of the grape. The cells below
are whitewashed cellars now, the bottles
ready as history. Shelved too long,
their crimson stains do not erupt
but rather, so slowly one might be dead

before, they brown and sour: their wet
becomes an acrid attack, and bitter
as lees after pressing. But that
seldom reaches the street. The old
is mouthed alone, or binds like blood

those who recall the Hotnot
who filled his throat in a vat,
was found after bottling, beneath the scraps
of leaf, the grit, insects and sweat
that make wine more than red.

THE CLOUD

While we slept, the cloud came:
we saw it hunched over town.
Just like a table-cloth, some said,
cameras aimed as it tested the height.
Next day it joined us: damp, white.
You couldn't open your mouth too wide –
we whispered. Then it stood on corners,
wondering where next or lost.
It got in the way of shoppers.
People offered it help, said good morning
– we're famed for hospitality – but no reply
or smile. A few protested, the way
people do about anything new.
It's a tourist attraction, the Council said,
and gave it the city's freedom. Their line changed
when it took to the streets, ate cars.
Only the few, never heard of again, could afford
special gasmasks, so we mostly stay home.
Used to speaking quietly, looking grey.
No red bleeding hearts here.
That's how we are.

CAPE COTTAGE SCENE

The Coloureds were kicked out of here,
she said, regarding the white walls
(damp-stains here & there)
& graphics, books above all.

Don't know what I'm meant to do.
Protest? Get out? She refused coffee
said she should go. Ja, they were also
stables & once zebras roamed, they say.

There's no neighing at night, tho.
& the Coloureds are flat somewhere.
No ghosts to write home about, nor
relics, just books & the

rot & blister of browning walls.
It's got to stop somewhere. Meanwhile,
you wanted to go. I'll sleep or read.
Hope night doesn't fall on my head.

SUBURBORAMA

Daily my life contracts. Once dreamt
of two suitcases packed in an hour,
a jet quivering in space and a new
expanse of blue skies, brown earth and
seas pure and light as a salt-grain.

But I have a cottage, furniture, job,
a servant to squeeze out the dirt.
There's a woman here whose ivy laughter
fills every room. And bills that stalk
through the mail-box, grow fat on stale verses.

At night, the salesmen flit.
I slam windows, lock doors, shove the woman –
heaving with joy – into a cupboard.
But in they burst, blossoming Carnegie smiles,
sprouting hands that demand shaking.

They're not come to sell anything,
only to offer me mortgages,
insurance, secure opinions on Life.
They'll accept in exchange the verses
that sang of injustice or simply girls
left sleeping at dawn, or electric serenity
of cats and nights treacled with talk.
O, they'll have the lot.

One morning I'll wake and breathe
cement and curl away from the sun
and cleave to the bulb that glares
and bores past marbling eyes.
And one morning when she brings me
Rice Crispies I'll not even ask how
she slept for the thousandth time
but blink Drink Coca-cola

Drink Coca-cola Drink Coca-cola
and open and shut open and shut
and I'll open and shut my mouth in a smile.

PARTIES

Bordering the blank solidarity of houses,
with Mustangs and Jags for sentries,
the jacarandas are innocuous greenery.
Yet, every spring, they gather their force
from grass roots and unclench in a mauve explosion.

You're always safe with nature, if
you know where it is. A part of me
shines among fair women, booming men
at parties, slides slick as a goldfish,
finning epigrams. And when Zonnebloem blooms
in serious bellies, our concern spreads
an epic of words, words, words
to block out the night.

But at my back, always that other,
sneering at family portraits and
dark as a fisherman seen from shallows.
He can't understand reasons or wit,
would rather dance than talk, and failing that,
hands drinks or announces dinner
or lurks with the night in the corner.

Till pressed. He seizes the machine gun
from its place on the mantelpiece
and sends the night, hot with stars,
through bodies softer than irony,
rips apart skins that dam honest blood.

But that's beyond the borders of reality.
There are jacarandas and houses. They stand
on common earth. That's nature, that's life.
My friends say they're keeping cool,
waiting for spring.

JUNIOR EXECUTIVE

Sit in the lounge and gaze at the view;
Ask the old man if he's read anything new;
Go home, eat spaghetti, just me and you:
    Life's always been life for us.

Take a lift at 7 sharp, catch a bus;
The wide-open newspapers say "Don't look at us";
Cough, don't whistle, spit, make a fuss:
    Life's always been keep off the grass.

Chat about Saturday night with the boys.
Back to work, here comes the boss.
Just like him we give work to the secretaries:
    Life's always been passing the buck for us.

And one has a cat, one's got a boyfriend;
one has her crochet that won't ever end,
and one has tits that point at the end:
    Life's always been mother's milk for us.

Work's not so great in the afternoon.
You dream of new houses by South Coast lagoons,
But the typewriters rattle, the telephones croon:
    Life's a Berea flat for us.

Home to the papers, home to the lies.
Not everything here is prison and spies
And anyway, what about overseas:
    Life's always been peaceful for us.

LEAVETAKING

The Management changed. Like the bed
of a winter stream, his desk was dusty.
On blotting paper he signed his name
Till they complained of the waste.

Slunk through the office at half-past eight,
Left like a spy at four;
They watched him stride with empty files
And a blush at the typist's leer.

"Not long now" – they'd seen it before;
"Reasons of space": the tactful departure
To a carpetless room on an upper floor.
(But the view, he said, was better there.)

The rest you know: days staring
At beckoning streets, the regretful smiles,
The hopes expressed, the hearty handshake
And no gold watch.

PROMISES

Come live with me & be my love
& I will order the elephants
to paint their toenails green & Banda
to clean your shoes every day
& the Voortrekker Monument I'll
send leaping like a holy cow
right over the moon as a gift
to the Martians. For you I'll see
that the baobabs dance 'Swan Lake'
in the park on Sundays you'll hear
how I taught the jacaranda blossoms
to sing in tune. For you
Vorster & Nelson will grin & bear
one another & play Tiddley-winks
in Robert Greig Square & if that
will not move you why then
I'll write you a serious poem a
sonnet an epic a praise song
each rime will be your name if
I learn how to spell it. If you
will not live with me & be my love
& if you only want to see
your mirror why then I'll bribe it
to pull tongues at you as I
do not & then my love I know
you will come & love with me
& be my till I drive you
home or mad.

THE ABORTION

Too late now to recriminate.
Appalled, each consulted friends.
One said she knew a doctor who might . . .
Love-making now didn't seem right.

Somehow they spoke less and less,
Knowing three months could be dangerous.
Rather the pain than marriage, she said,
But she still loved him, she confessed.

Told himself it had been worth it,
Solicitous as a husband, tense
As a murderer. "It happens
If you're careless" was all her parents said.

They understood, took the cheque, gave consent.
That night he spent with a girl
He screwed on and off. She wouldn't get pregnant –
He'd ensured she was on the pill.

When he called with flowers,
She was loving and pale in bed.
No need for the solemn face,
She laughed. Inside he was dead.

"Yes, a bit of blood – not painful.
Feel – my breasts are all milky."
Swollen eyes. "Was it a boy or a girl?"
He did not expect her to cry.

LOVE POEM

To write a love poem
first you must burn her letters
razor away her face from the photo
now the frame
take up your laser and move
like a surgeon or soldier
remove her name from agates,
clear afternoons and the like

now open your mouth gasp and train
the ray on your brain: the parts
that scream must be martyrs if you
are to write a love poem.

Now where her fingers touched
cut. Nose, the toothbrush, carpets.
She must go too, you know that:
tell her it happened to Laura
Beatrice and Juliet. Others too,
and gently consign her to space
that waits at the window.
If this is to be a love poem
there should be space now.
In time it will thicken like a scar
of dried blood, in time she will grow
as full as a page
of words.

THE UNICORN

There *are* unicorns.
I haven't seen them myself
but others have, reliable men
who write in books, in newspapers.
Once, travellers told
of blue-eyed unicorns with barber's pole horns
that raced in deserts, visited virgins in dreams.
There's even talk of a unicorn
that walked down Adderley Street,
through a department store,
and speaking a mixture of English and Greek,
ordered nectar at the milk bar.
Someone asked for its autograph;
a father, eyeing that horn,
hauled his daughter away;
an elderly woman, beneath a black hat,
wanted to call Someone:
"It looks like a foreign idea".
(The unicorn sniffed its coke).
Then the men from the Natural History Museum came.

They wanted to see its skeleton,
said it was a kind of horse
and people said yes, they are Authorities after all,
which is why no-one actually saw
the unicorn.

KINGFISHER

You slid like smoke
above the river
and without stopping scooped a fish
from its grey dream of worms.
Now, with your drooping silver moustache,
you fluff at other birds:
would pull a tongue
if you were less hungry.

Now, winged knife,
you should be an emblem of our politicians
as you wonder how to swallow
all your too much
without choking,
over-balancing
or losing any to any other.

Next. How will you fly again?

CREATION

That still day,
Whales toiled the swell
Of the bold Atlantic, spume
Cast like bones between
Sea and sky.

Slipped like a shell
From cold, italic breakers,
Stunned by a primal sun,
I slept. Knew earth
That harboured.

A man intruded:
Ankles black and taut,
Eyes obscure as a snake's.
He offered me crayfish, brawling
And semaphoring in a bag.

His eyes transfixed.
Menaced by his words, I grew
Brittle as the lurching crayfish,
Eyes lagooned in blood. Drawn
Into his skin, his storms,

Yet snared by my unfurling
In the sun, I was remote.
Relieved, I watched him
Dwindle like a flame.

And now, blanched as a shell
Flayed in waves, choked
In quicksands of days,
Escape might confirm flesh,
Restore breath.

AGAINST NATURE

Do not stroll in gardens
or greenhouses or gaze too closely
at flowers. You will feel the mound
of earth in your stomach heave
out of the walls of your skin,
your fingers will curl like tendrils,
your hair turn green and seek the wind
if you stroll in gardens or greenhouses,
or lose yourself in a flower's scent.

They warned about water,
whether waiting in rivers, oceans, lakes
or taps, keep clear of water or
your blood will breach its banks,
saliva tide with the moon's tug
and your eyeballs unwind like streams

you will run and run like a tap
if you cannot keep clear of water.

And fire, which licks you
into shape, keep it far
if you want to be full.

You cannot turn yourself to stone
for stone will split and turn to earth;
you cannot freeze yourself to ice
for ice will melt and bear you off:
Change yourself to neutral steel
that flame and grass and water fear,
change yourself to shiny steel –
you'll never die or live.

THE OPERATION

Rising that morning through the pain,
I entered a clean, white world.
But in the night,
a faceless man, with sleep
slim and silver in his hand
had cut them off, my
different feet, given me an anchor.
He called my plasters "bedsocks";
they'd keep me still
for a while.
I almost turned head over heels
looking and saw that russet
spreading on the sole.
So they'd moved my heart –
it was trying to go
to my feet in the ashcan.
No, no, they're there, people said,
underneath, cocooned to protect
the wings.
Who else had wings?
They tried to sign their names
on the plasters. Each night
I wiped off their hands
that were beneath me.

Then the shears came,
moving slow mandibles, cracking
cocoons. The wings flaked off
like scaly skin
when the air got in.
I studied walking.

LESSON IN WALKING

Take your feet for granted.
If you ask how such bulk is so
narrowly based how can they go?
Trust. Don't emulate dancers
or athletes yet: they'll only
make you weight. Now focus on ground
see if it's visible, sloping or bare,
keen to hold you or hole you in one
to Australia but believe it's benign
as a farmer too busy with growing
to bother with hikers like you. Stand.
Not too long lest the wind
prey on your limbs. Believe me
this walking has hazards. Lift from a heel
and lean and before you fall, lift
from a heel and now take your feet for
granted but not the ground: don't
part too long or you'll belong
nowhere and that's lesson one walking.
Tomorrow you'll lift a bit longer
from heels, learn taking the ground
for granted – that's lesson two
flying.

AFTER READING BISHOP BERKELEY'S
"PRINCIPLES OF HUMAN KNOWLEDGE"

Choose your clues: a chair in a quad,
unicorn, acorn, toenail or bomb – no matter.
This bottle. Been around a bit: it

can't take heights. A daisy will make
you fast: it won't last the week:
something is at it. Use your eyes
and remember you can't work at night,
they're slower than light
though adept at lying.
Finally words: they'll send you straying
to a chair in a quad, unicorn, acorn,
toenail or bomb. They're all you've got
cling on
till they break like breccia.
The job we don't know. Try anyway.
I believe it's something to do with
it's something to do with
something to do with or something.
If you fail, you fail.
If you succeed, we'll make you patron
of the Society for Psychic Research.
Now march.

DIGGING

Once at the seashore, knowing no better
I thought the whole world rested on water
For pawing the sand a short depth, how
wetness rose among the brown grains! It lay
alive in its still hole, an eye
that granted repose to what was mirrored.
But if I did not care, then back sand
slipped and soaked it through, or someone
wanting reasons would kick the water out,
saying people might tumble in and drown.
It's the same now, and knowing people say
I'm blood, gristle and bone and more than
water underlies us. And that is why
now and then I clear a space within
where water or whatever can lie, be seen
free of sharks or storms. Not for long
enough to hurt anyone though.
I say "It's people": that could be. But maybe
it's me that shifts, then the edges blur
and crumble into grit. There's no being sure

50

never, not even when people or whatever
put sand on top of your coffined head
to soak it up. I don't know better.

A VISIT TO THE INSTITUTION

Getting out there is no problem, a pleasure
to drive with windows wide to the day's exhalation
of sunlight. And once there, the horizon
lopes into the sky. Only if you were
above it all could subterranean flexing be seen.
Here she spends her nights. We stroll
and crackle across the wintry lawn,
remembering to turn approaching the wall,
not to mention children somewhere beyond,
or whatever might peck into her face. All
is still, I agree, and especially the pond
Whose flaccid water has stunned the goldfish.
You get used to the people and the food's OK.
She doesn't invite me to stay, not that I wish
to, passing a palm tree that spurts from razor-leaves
the dark and red quarrelling of birds.

BURGLARS

As if the ground could lurch
and send us sprawling, we pick our path
through night. The alarm must be choked
before it daubs the sky with its red yell.
Once we hoped that burglars would avoid
the lights of domesticity then
we stumbled on their disregard.
Burglars are scared of the dark
and pick a path through dark
to found a home from ours.
Perhaps inside they fear the floor
might claw them down or sirens call
them out. I know life would be calmer
without all this and they'd agree

but there are walls and doors with voices,
night without and night within, and now
is a matter of finding the key,
loudly enough for them to leave
but not too loudly: they may take fright,
leave us to sleep through the dawn.

SETTLERS' STORY

I

The island squats.
Grass pierces sand
and rips the venturing hand.
Waves rebel, clawing the child.
We sleep armed,
distrust the timorous guard
and dream of home.

II

Confined by the island,
we are free to reject
northern seasons that rhythmed poems.
We hide from the vigilant sun
that strips and explodes pale skin.
we recoil from our flesh;
the kisses of snarling lips;
and bilious fruit and fish.
Words peel and harden
to teeth of flint. Groping,
we prey and confirm isolation.

III

Rocks liquefy in light
yielding gold to barren breasts.
Bones of the mythical lion
nourish our soil;
the sea acquiescent urges
flowering masts to foreign lands.
Our sons flourish, pallid as termites.

IV

Once, resisting our passions,
the island confirmed us.
We reel from the plough.

WATERMELON BREAKFAST

Green rind,
dark pink flesh glistening
grainy trail
on your face as if
you gave up washing lipstick
halfway.
And the pips
the pips should be mentioned,
the way they speckle the fruit
are left stranded
boats without masts
when their red ocean
slides down the throat.
New they shine on the plate:
if we left them long enough,
they'd harden.

Take thread
exchange them for balding chickens
on a hot day
ochre ground
hard as bare feet
the dust lifting
the flies falling
a sharp smell of sweat,
and there, far away, the hills
faint as green rinds
deliquescent
the sea, the Indian ocean.
If you look hard,
how the sharks rip that blue
apart. If they were large
or not stunned by the day,
you would see the water
fall apart in chunks

and the sharks
neat in their shells, black
watermelon pips.

And what about the chickens?
The kraal, the sharks, the ocean?
Surely this leads somewhere?

The chickens? Stringy.
The kraal? Bulldozed.
The houses pus on the hills.
But the ocean is learning ways
to stick together.
That's another country.
They eat the rinds there, down to the quick.

The watermelon, back to the watermelon.
Now all that sweet pulp's gone
except for the trail on your chin.
All that's left are two green cuticles
thirty black pips.
We'll string them together in amulets
to ward off the ghosts
and start again, sharing
the vast, arced smile
of wet watermelons.

DRUNK AT THE BLIND PIG, ANN ARBOR, MICHIGAN

The boy from Georgia:
hey man wheredjuh git that lightuh?
From Africa, come from Africa.
Had friends in Kenyuh,
kinda neauh Ashuh,
maybe neauh Pretoria?
The music men came, you know Louisiana?
Hitting the table, drinking the beer.

So many places we been together
on the roads all kinds of weather.
And the round night out there,

and somewhere's Penelope – planes on the skyway –
somewhere's the surfers in far California.

And her trying to talk through the music
into my ear.
I'd like to smile but I can't hear
you dear.

When I wanted you, you weren't there:
now you want me, I just couldn't care.

You smile but it turns out a leer
and when I come close, your eyes disappear.

Circe.
Trying to turn me on with your dancing:
we were last out of there,
the stars hurling about you wanted to piss
unpeeled almond trying to turn me on
smiling, dribbling. The sirens scraping
the streets like a womb.

And when you've finished squatting
leap away right over the moon
and I'll ride the bike home
pretend to be sleeping when you come in
randy and crazy.

LAST SUPPER, WITH RATATOUILLE AND
CALIFORNIAN WINE

Take eggplants.
Prefer aubergines, mauve of negro aureolas.
At the drug-store buying wine, black guy:
aw man, buy me brandy got no ID.
Split with my bread, the bastard.
Slice aubergines, Uncle Toms, white inside.
Fry in flour.

Take green peppers,
succulent caves. The pips burn.
Six of us cooking: Bill eyeing her,

I'm free, off to California in the morning.
Been a carpenter after Vietnam, been
most states, seen things people move on.
She glances at him
stripping cherries for a bowl
of red eyesballs. Slice green peppers,
marrows, onions (eat bread, no tears)
salt, arrange in layers.

Open California wine.
The Gallo's sour, leave it alone –
they screw their workers. Home too.
We tried protest, we tried violence
they got guns. No point getting uptight:
they'll die first and if they join us great.
Hitching Wisconsin way, rednecks too scared
to ask about my hair. They're a minority.
Home theybe Prime Minister say sir
bastards. Don't let people hassle you:
open red California wine,
off to California in the morning.

Bake and eat.
Talk over country music and tricky Dick
on TV looks real sick and you
playing games   off to Cal-
asking him to your room   -ifornia
should've moved my things   in the
long ago guess you're a person   morning
not a lay and I won't go up next
though we're young and you reckon
talking won't free you, no
way. I'm off to California in the morning,
drinking California now.

THE REUNION

You touched my arm, and from
that fusion we moved in grace,
though you touched my arm a last time.

I asked you why and you replied:
the time I limped in a gown all black.
Did you find that sad or weird?

But our love forgot that –
our beginnings are buried:
your hand grew away, layered

with skins the way a tree is.
The one I knew on mine cracked
and now it nourishes

the clasping wood in this new
embrace. My gown is furled too,
it has no claims on me or you.

I do not limp anymore. That all lies
in a cupboard below the stairs
somewhere behind, with designs for a house

never built, save in the mind.
Even that is not true: do you remember how
we found a house in Illovo ruined,

only the stone humped in rows?
Just the arbour was left, awry
where roses spurted through the grass,

the yellow and white cosmos, the shards
of wine bottles smashed by tramps.
Sullen, they watched us colonise yards

of a house strong in words. Or maybe
I went with my sister? Or perhaps I dreamed
rising from sharp green anaesthesia?

You say no, you didn't go there,
not with me. You remember the night
in the suburbs, clasped in a car, where

Alsatians snarled in the hedges. And staring
over my shoulder, or through my head
you saw servants lope by, daring

the curfew. You tell how one
thought our car was a Black Maria.
I didn't see him stare or run.

You see the fugitive behind my shoulder,
I choose the ruined garden. Both ways
that season is over,

even its ghosts stare past one another.
All night we have tried
to meet in this room, where the floor

tracks every move like radar:
your cats' heads turn, priming their claws,
your plants drown the sun in green water.

I could easily sink, like a broken gull
into the humus of kelp,
meet you there in a green swell.

But one day I'd wake, pared to an eye
reflecting a final view of sky, though
you clasped me till sea turned dry.

And for you to rise and disarm
your hydras, to leave the room
where words plummet and stun – what harm?

But I've seen you in gardens, in sun,
how your skin is aghast at the light,
it splits, how blood will not come.

Now only the small Atlantic parts us
and rolls at our common coasts.
I gave your gardens, gowns and this poem,

you return me your hand, that fugitive season.
All these we jettison now: I know
nothing there is more certain

than letting eyes graze on the ocean.
As one morning, past bathers and mountains
mine hooked on the dolphin

that leapt and arched
and took the eyes five feet under
then rose again and again, one matched

by another in arabesques that inscribed
the air I shared, the sea
with their momentary fusion.

THE NEW HOUSE

The Lounge
A bay window needs a window seat
where you can spy on the street
spying on you. Instead I have
two chairs and a couch. A door
leads in, one out. That out
is used most: the room is poised
like a host expecting guests. The chairs
are too stiff to clasp me there:
they're shocked by the move, her going.
We've something in common.

The Study
My past is filed.
What I want is there,
what I want to forget
need not be found.
The books will say anything
I need to hear
and the pictures wait to be looked at:
they don't stare.
When I turn, the rusbankie is ready,
a place of shelter
and so would the study be
but there's a window: across the road
the neighbours are chatty as humans
and the door, I've learned,
won't stay closed but swings
like a compass needle wide.
By taking it off, it could be mended
but there's no point, except

the way it aims at the window,
the half-a-curtain or beyond.

The Bathroom
I keep meaning to close the window,
preserve the heat. Not much here,
sometimes enough to fuzz the mirror.
Closing my eyes, I hope to see
lianas loop from the ceiling,
vermilion orchids blaze on the wall
and yellow lilies lap on the banks
of a coffin-shaped bath where I lie
every night, meaning to close the window.

The Lavatory
Still I can turn
water to colour of stein;
with a few unmagical grunts
make earth from nothing.
This room is simple, purposeful, private:
I know what I am sitting here
it's what I will always be.
And – has the cistern a soul?
The way it empties, fills, empties seems human.

The Bedroom
Has an absent look. From the chair,
a man could be refuelled on the luminous skin
of a woman dressing. I don't know
why it's here. The wardrobe is steel, upright:
it wandered in from the kitchen,
and the bed is a bed: it can summon
sleep from the world's four corners.

The Kitchen
Here is food and water.
I drink and eat alone,
keep it clean till my face
blurs white in the shiny stove.
There's no fridge: I don't
need ice – the arctic of glass
supplies the room, though not
that cylindrical jar where gaudy bananas
thrash and brawl their way to the brim.

One day they'll get out,
chopped into cereal one cold morning.

The Garden
The garden can wait.
The peach tree will spin off its leaves,
the grass keep green. Nothing I do
can bleach the brown soil nor make
it darken. The garden is safe:
all around are white bricks
which the ground bears kindly
hoping, one day, they'll be taken in.
Above every evening, the swoop
and susurrus of wheeling wings
and as they turn, they lead the light
away. One day, they'll curvet low,
flood the garden, flow through the house
their sky. That day, like the garden,
must wait. I must clear a way inside.

Between Islands

MIKE KIRKWOOD

Mike Kirkwood was born in St Vincent, West Indies
in 1943. He is married, has three children and
lectures in the Department of English at the University
of Natal, Durban. He is one of the editors of
Bolt Magazine.

CONTENTS

Acknowledgements are due to: *The London Magazine, The Purple Renoster,*
Bolt, Concept and *Ophir.*
Copyright © Mike Kirkwood 1975

BETWEEN ISLANDS

My father shuttled through those islands,
the war over, his youth thirsty for an immortal
pickling in rum. We made the schooner passage from Trinidad
back to St Vincent, in weather he remembered a long time.
The belly of that ship was black as cottonseed,
smelling of oiled planks, the bedded mainmast groaning.
Having no thoughts I did not think *the sea will split us.*
Around me were household spirits: mother, a black nurse, two scared
   sisters,
fathers' surgical knives rattling loose in their black casings.

CONVERSATION WITH A HURRICANE

I was down the other side of the island,
the day it headed our way, with my mother's people.
Grandfather turned up the atmospherics on his set,
and made us listen. *You can hear every word she's saying.*
I thought all the jumbies in the Caribbean were on our track.
When he got the bulletin he said, *We got to get in our hole.*
His carpenter Abraham marched the plantation people in,
two by two like the ark, three by three like the slave ship,
while grandmother looked her last on all God had given her.
Inside, she sat straightback in the only chair
and commanded the people to sing, softly
charming the boo-hoo and screech from the crackling air,
till grandfather said, 'You can bet she's missing us,'
and, 'Abraham, you can take these folks up out of here.'

RAS TYBJI

Calcutta coolie, contemptible fellow
in whose eyes love and fear were doves
endlessly pursuant in a kind of rapture
your famous cousin had a better head for
(a scaler of silk ropes, unveiler of mango trees),
you drew from your Trinidad sahib the worst
kindnesses, condescensions, and spurious affections
any ex-Ghoorka officer ever bestowed

on so appealingly beautiful a batman of sad eyes.
Thrown over for Miss Fresitas (this young lady's father
was a Portuguese fish-merchant, and her mother had
a touch of colour; she herself was considered a beauty)
you made a hash of murder, but a better job
of suicide in the cocoa grove. Miss Fresitas
gave a little scream and clung to Captain Sefton
while you hovered there, waiting for the last time,
your rope-thin legs well clear of the ground,
an old soiled glove of Sefton's pressed to your chest,
while the ground glass you meant for their coffee
was received and classified a curiosity
in the police archives, Port 'o Spain, there
with a yellowing tag and its slur of a story
to wait the coming of long knives, brickbats, stens.

DURBAN VERANDAHS

I
The Old Lady's, On The Ridge
A sharp-eyed old lady at the top
looking down her long dim verandah
or up at her tall dry palms
says, 'Once our nearest neighbour was'
– jerking away the town with her thumb –
'where the greek is on that corner.'
Measuring the long stone verandah
perambulations of her chair
recall a generous hand her father had
who built when the young green palms
could still tempt a dry old elephant out
of the uncleared dark garden-end.

II
The Mouse of Parliament's, Half-way up
Our member of parliament, whose sons
performed in turns upon the school piano
has pushed his verandah out a bit
to sink the cocktail-hour overflow
or float, perhaps, two high-backed chairs
he planed himself from local wood:
in one he dwindles to little pointed knees

and large hands, the other brims all over
full of his copious wife, whose admiration stands
in spate self-fed by all about her,
the mice she suckled and the Mouse she made.

III
Moonsamy Govender's, Down the Hill
White frangipani, pink oleander
flower about drunken Moonsamy Govender
and his attendant train, loser's tickets
on all six races, empty half-jack of GV,
a half-torn programme for City in the Cup.
He sweetens with frangipani in the dust
and dreams himself in oleander leaves.
His wife leans on the wooden balustrade
but not too heavily, hears above on tin
first lax rhythms of a summer rain
and ponders whether she should lug him in.

IV
The Road
Elephants made it, a dry old lady
remembers wagon-ruts, our Mouse
has squeaked his squeak to push it out
a bit, Moonsamy Govender's youngest brother
once swept it, sharp eyes and a long broom.
Morning and evening it tides full
outside my door, throb of buses
bearing in each morning, bearing out
dark hats, strange careless men,
bright scarves, reverberative women
whirled in an alien, tired artery.

An old lady's watchful eye,
a dwindled mouse in mouse's hole
– a hill uprooted, burrowed out,
corseted with garden walls,
unthreatened by elephants
might fall entirely from itself
(borne up by that throbbing pulse)
to frangipani Govender in the dust
lying in wait for a summer rain.

OLD BIG MOUTH

Campbell just stood there blazing away.

Even when the last pale punk of his enemy
no longer affronted him – the hat of the vaquero
and the flash cape holding the hill to a man,

entranced yet perfectly able to whistle
up the requisite soldierly indifference
no doubt – still that voice, admiration

screaming like blood in his ears, maybe
even the voice of that cousin sergeant from whom
he rifled accent, gestures, a few good stories,

coming up to him from below, out of the ranks
attentive to their Ridge Rd. Olympian,

that big mouth of his has blown up more
than the echo of his own bullied fame,

taken the legs off any trick-shooter
lowering his sights in the vicinity.

HENRY FYNN AND THE BLACKSMITH OF THE GROSVENOR

I
Bones sleeping in the cove – toes tight
in gullies, the sweet dreams of skulls
tucked under the sandy coverlet,
a jaw-bone braying where the swells

whiten and hiss the reef – I sing
not these first dead, the Indiaman's
quiet clerk or termagant bosun
sitting out the sea's stiff dance;

not the remaindered mythic band
who made eight hundred miles on prayer,
the flesh of oysters, limpets and
others who lost their grip, it's feared;

not those left propped up in caves,
nor the sunburned virgins with eyes
brighter than beads, whose blood still leaves
pallor on a tribesman's features;

but you, blacksmith, who chose to stay,
and by the time the last sleeve waved
or hat lifted where the long bay
turns, had hefted, hurled and heaved

pig-iron of the ship's ballast
up the beach with a realist's hands.
On that cliff-top your forge flame faced
out the tough sea, a continent's

tougher customers, the trials
by conscience, women, work
and the casual round of wars
you made your life by. And your luck

held, which was all you hoped; months, years.
Shipwrecks of kraals, extinguished tribes,
and lost scouts behind whom all ways
went thorny with spears, came to your fire.

II
Fifty years on came Fynn, starving,
living from root to root, begging
at hovels and hide-outs from skins
already too stretched and staring

to shrink from any new horror.
This was after Shaka's impis
had been that way and back. Further
north, over his morning coffee

on the beach, alone, his two guides
sweating somewhere in the undergrowth,
Fynn had watched the army glide
incuriously by; in his throat

Shaka, the charm sounded over
and over, while they passed so close,
twenty thousand shield to shoulder,
he sat all morning in one place.

69

Light-headed from his month of hunger,
Fynn thought he'd found the Grosvenor's gold
when iron outcrops made him stumble
in long grass growing through the forge

or where the forge had been, but soon
mastered the truth: saw with calm blows
a new day's sun driven to its noon,
ship's ballast lying straight in rows.

SUGAR SUNDAY

I
A mad blue wind is blowing, the smiler
whose grin lasts days; a speechless gull is rocked
miles inland with specks of sand and sea-salt;
a beak, eyes needle the green depths of cane;

by thousand on thousand, impeccably
massed and squared on the small coastal hills
of Umdloti, Tongati, Umhlali tilting northward,
march the infallible green impis waving

southward to the mouth of Durban where Umgeni
spreads her lap to salmon and drowned seamen,
by the densely fleshed parade and the city's
banks, car-marts, anciently rapacious drapers,

and beyond to the terminal's twin silos,
each perfected by a tit of white gold
untouched by human hand nestling roof-high
in the clasp of its stainless-steel voluptuary,

while slowly between bluff and breakwater
a long belly slides in, sounds as of ghosts
cheering in the riveted steel hollows.

II
Sunday, and after lunch the young manager
new-married, heavy with food, dreamily watched
by a wife too much of a girl to know
how much she is appalled (left to stand there

in her successful vegetable garden)
goes out to shoot monkeys. He leaves the truck
hidden in cane, mounting the long green swells
to where a bearded cliff of bush maroons
those castaways. And back across a stalled
silence his shots drag echoes as he aims
at wisps that rive and weave the wilderness.
Small birds fly up, a hah di dah mounts and wheels
in compulsive clamour on its course, blood
is dripping into the brush here and there
mixing with sap from torn sprigs and leaves
where the bough still jerks under a grey writhe
tightening to dead-weight. Later, in the pile
of loosened fur and estranged faces
on the truck-back, she remarks the hands
that clasp a chest, hold a pink stain
there as delicately as a baby.

III
Sunday, and shoals of chrome reflections rise
troubling a gull's flight with swoops, with shivers
over the warm tar-swell: sleepy drivers
wrap their minds in slowly somersaulting
infinite green cocoons, entered only
by the saving shrills of children, or a wife's
phlegmatic elbow. Behind such seekers
after the unspoilt bay, the perfect wave,
the velvet sand which mantles whalebones not
sardines tins, a breathless low-church Sunday;
platitudes of a bald ten o'clock sun
muzzle the roots of lawn-grass, pink roof-tiles
tick and click closer to noon like prayers,
electric intercessions on the heads
of convential cats clawing empty beds,
rooms, whole sabbath suburbs.

At half-past two in the sugar heartland
a sleeping legavaan snaps up his head,
and a mile away a cane-rat scurries;
a manager's wife hears the faint steel wailing
but thinks it is her heart and doesn't wonder;
the sky is empty of stray gulls, butterflies,
everything; the wind tears at the blue hole;
wagon-trains of cars pull over and wait,

surrendered to speculating grandmothers;
through fat canelands the sleek white ambulance races.

BOERS

I
Going north, up by Weenen
and Majuba, such places,
I, with old generals, dawdled
in fields of bone-shard, bullets,
spurs that may still urge a line
of advance as ants decide.
Around here, too, on cold days
in the first rains, loud as ice
run rivers of stone and blood.

II
Taking your stand in the *kroeg*
in a dorp like Warden, when
two or three beers on, the worst
of the drive recedes (ribbed cows
restless among mealie stalks,
sheep grey as rats in stale fields,
and the whole Transvaal smoking)
you may wake to Koos de Wet
or Generaal de la Rey
crowding your elbow. Until
at two removes of plate-glass
you notice the burgher wives
plotting in the supermarket,
hear *bitter-einder* voices
vowing death to Peter Hain.
On the way out of Warden
a tractor with rickets
and no paintwork oozes oil
into dust-drifts on the stoep
of an abandoned seed-store.

III
When every spoor, the wagon
-creases on the one blank page
of veld I stared on, staled,

some Tswanas, out on a hunt
with curs that sneaked through the ribs
of lands yielding one rabbit
to the acre, told me this:

Go to Mothopo water,
to Makalakala where
the ash-coloured ones were caught,
Makopye the Boer's people,
he of the jutting forehead,
the red-faced man who fled.

And there, close by the hillock
of Silologae, where stones
still rear and hold the country
round it massively at bay,
I found you, Harklaas Malan,
still leaning against one wheel
of an upturned splintered cart,
your eyes blazing up the road
to nowhere your survivors took,
mouth set to the long grimace
of possessing history.

IV
In early day I first
went out after one. The dust
in the Old Fort gardens gave
nothing away, but cycads
there opined they'd never come.

The old gaol like a black bird,
like a mynah crudely nests
among loose railway-ends.

From beyond, on slow ferries,
the city consigned its sounds.

Board-room blague was minuted
in secretarial snickering
at Collingsby, Coombe, and Co.

Somebody's cover-drive
reverberated off the splice:

around the stupefied ground
a sudden trot of cavalry;
and, in Field Street, the presses
registering adulation.

Behind moustaches, gulch-hats,
the long stares of their rifles,
ride the remote or sudden
-ly asleep swarthy faces
retreating to photographs.

Then coming again, almost
clear of the last surfaces.

GULLIVER'S DAY

The sun this morning, hours before you woke,
through blinds, the pallid sheet, a senseless skin,
staked out your giant heart and slowed its stroke.

Staggered, your will inched from toes to hair-roots.
Dreams clear. Your blood is swampland. On the floor
sly sunbeams and cockroaches in cahoots,

small yachts incline to tankers in our bay.
The skyline buildings have made fast your limbs,
the streets reach up like ropes. Still, it's your day,

the first of summer. Our mayor, costumed
as a lifey and flanked by Roy Campbell
and Barry Richards (all three gents consumed

by a civil embarrassment), climbs your chest
conferring certain freedoms. When they've gone
and the man from the *Mercury* has guessed

how much each pendant testicle outweighs
a cricket-ball, a paw-paw, or his own,
there will be time to punish and to praise

before, letting curious Lilliput be,
you struggle into baggies, grab a towel,
and sleepwalk down to face the gathering sea.

RAIN

Black Sundays. When bees tick over in the roof
and the honey stain continues in the ceiling.
When the rain perforates the air and admits
no new sounds. When our lives pile up
and children build tents in the blankets.

Love days. We kept the house, not ours,
open as we found it to others. Didn't dare
shake a curtain that from the street
might have seemed to close on a pact.
Left all the lights off, so the trees
could push their dark in.
Slipped through doors that frowned
or looked bored, till we found
a room love could unpack in.

ROOT GATHERERS

A magnezium moon flashes
flesh from the hill-top skeletons.

The burnt-out cottage. Trees drowning in the gale. Grass spooking head
   high.
Sockets of boulders the valley sucked down one wet year.

Flitting through holes, with a pick, with a sack,
two muthi men stalk suburbia. Stare down on its starry winking.

The high ululations of dogs, dreams
of bland healthy children, distant conceivings
of area committees yawn to admit them.

The pick plunges, finding the earth soft and sticky.
The sack swells.

BOROUGH FRINGES

I
Out this way someone is delivering
houses. Every three months another
half-dozen arrive.
                    Double garages
spawn and are about to gulp
the houses.
                    Grass starts to creep
over the blanks of quarter-acre plots.

An age of Alsatians, Dobermans
and Great Danes dawns. The garages
regress to kennels, a plasticised fence
inherits each house.
                    And now Volkswagens
begin to mate in the driveways.

II
In late September the first big rains
are allocated. Factory effluents
foam the gullies, and well-greased eels
make cross-country moves at night.

My car has a mournful catarrh and I walk home.

I see sinkholes in most of the lawns
and crazed concrete strips careening
up eroded drives. A marooned
anxiety wells in the throats of dogs.

As usual I see no-one, not counting
stray blacks and children, one itinerant
burlesqueing hawker of straw brooms

and you, old snow-top gallivanter
whose saucer of a smile balances
apple-cheeks of Amsterdam, trotting
your knickety-knock of a mare
around our shaky perimeter.

NEIGHBOURS

Over your shoulder you throw ropes
of raw earth down the scrub, snaring
the thickets in loops, letting down
tenuous travellers, herdboys, cows.

The vlei between us is no man's.

Vigilant, I pump in ten rounds
of golf ball a day, and patrol
my hillside for the spent casings.

The herdboys also play, with clubs
sawn-off and hickory-shafted,
teeing on tufts the balls I lose.

Back at home, I'm learning Zulu,
Radio Bantu at peak volume,
ready to receive your envoy.

You send down a *tsotsi* with a knife,
and call me at dusk to the vlei,

send down his interpreter, who squats
in a bloodied shirt explaining
a ten-cent slot under the heart,

the ambulance a long time coming.

OLD SALT

Sedated by breakwaters and today's
mild westerly, your ocean gives itself
up quietly to seven city beaches.

The room they've given you on the 14th floor
is all windows. All your visitors look out
and give you, over their shoulders, bulletins
on seabirds, shipping, the weather, surfing form.

You pretend to read the papers, never leave the bed,
knowing to the last fathom how much water is out there.

Today I count a dozen ships queueing in the anchorage.
Every couple of hours a tug comes, and another one goes in.

THE GAMBLERS

Every Wednesday I bring you
a race-card, and by Saturday morning,
in and out of absences, you've filled in
the stray crosses of one more permutation.

You have to tell me where to go, without surprise
that after fifteen years I still don't know.
In there, I'm helpless in the crush
of steady losers, maintaining your claim
in the records of the arithmeticians of odds.

On Monday our ticket goes to the wash
in the back pocket of my jeans. Set out to dry,
then brown and brittle as an old gum leaf,
your selection's still decipherable. They'd pay us out

if we'd won, but neither of us looks to see.
On Wednesday the Greek pats my hand across the counter,
gives me a sure thing with Saturday's card.

SPARRING PARTNERS

Your hands stay big. You curl them to mime
the punch-drunk's weave and roll when I ask how you are.

Puzzled, your fists circle, look at each other
from crags of wrist. From there to the shoulders
you're nothing. You watch your arms
suddenly flutter to the bed, the hands spreading
to emergency landings on the empty arena of your chest.

A CITY DOCTOR

There's no-one to tell. Dying without friends
doesn't make you or anyone else sad.
You were lover of the sea and five or six maritime cities,
of which this was the last. I study the wrinkles
and cambered soles of your last pair of size thirteens;
take your old Ford out of the basement garage,
and cruise the seafront with salt filming the windscreen.

We seem to stop by appointment here and there,
seeing a barman you once knew coming off the pier
with a small catch of shad in a potato sack.
I try to picture, the way city people do, his family sitting to supper,
if he has a family. He nods. I put the parking lights on,
and buy a paper; head for the harbour to finish your round.

AT THE CAFÉ MOUSEL

At the Café Mousel, two worlds,
two round tables. One spins with wine,
cards, and slow, sour cigarettes.
The other, burnt out, gives no sign.

Yet a man sits there, and he stares
as at some puzzle in his hands
huddled on the bare, stained surface.
Then, on the stroke of two, he stands.

A NIGHT TRAIN

When, half-way through the sleep of an
old city, not your own, you come to
a moment in thought when words come
slowly off the page, and now a mind
tired but stripped to the work will
hold its mark, and begin very casually to

as down tracks
of its own
until that moment forgotten
familiar nightmare,
accelerating dangerously,
a night train passes.

THE DRUNK IN BLACKOUT

A lost world. No more his suns
melt in the glass. Oceans drain from the dead tubes,
his elemental visions.

Continents grind under his feet.
The stonewalk plates, buckled and slant as old tombs,
crust the new shores of a street.

Headlights shed some scaly gleams.
A fire-engine's fanfare is the scream of gill-hooked fish
winched up, flapping, from fathoms.

Taken in charge by the motherly lamp-post,
he clutches at her skirts.
The blind lead the blind up that abandoned coast.

THE NEW MEN

("The priests decided that the chief of the strange visitors
in these unprecedented ships was one of their own gods . . . . ."
Williamson: *Cook and the Opening of the Pacific*.)

All night your fires tongued
the fragrant wood of prophecies.
These were the dead returning.

Still sitting on the sea
at dawn, the paradisal bird.
Folded its cloud-pinions.

Into the longboat we took
a radiance unspoiled by storms.
The fired flesh of the dead.

At the first feasting
your king hid in the shadows,
his daughters at their dancing.

How could he tell them
not to dance the old dances?
Having seen a new sign

In the sky at mid-day,
in our captain's eyes.
Ash. The burnt-out past. He harboured

ghosts, a future's bleak conquistadores.

OF MOUNT ABORA

It was this waitress, in a place
Where *Morning Coffee* was the bait
For pastries lazing on the trays:
Her downcast eye, her dogged gait,

Her shoulders dipping through the stir
As here, then there, she served her stint,
Had half-bemused a traveller
Of cool and Aethiopian mint.

Three times she threaded through the maze
of tables; still he seemed bereft;
At last he smiled and dropped his gaze,
Shrugged, stretched, paid the bill, and left.

BETWEEN OURSELVES

A pit yawns under our talk:
each evening, a new subsidence,
the words slipping helplessly further away.

We look at each other across
the gap no-one's responsible for.
In the old days – fifty, a half dozen
years ago – we knew how to blame
each other, the krulkop calling
the kafferboetie black, an old joke
no-one now would care for. Instead each
in his thought circles an identical
and rueful vacancy, and we wait
on midnight to cry or cackle in it.

(FABLE: 1)

(In a folktale) there was
this king happy etc. but
one small thing he never
had seen the sun rise
        bothered him

The solid-gold palace
seemed an anchor you could
trust & so with grappling
hooks his guards made bold
        to hold down the sun

One morning early this
old woman under-burnisher
of the summer ballroom waited
head-down where the postern
        had been for years

& then looked up it was
she used to tell the little
children of the time that came
of all the marvels of the time before
        the most magnificent

(FABLE: 2)

O king be pleased to con
most puissantly this scroll
here be update statistics
sire here be thy sun's
    millenial points

and here the curve of his
invisible decline to shew
thy will is worked for sire
we own no doubt of thy
    immortal flourishing

cascading trumpets and
a long blast on the horn then
bland assurance of the strings but
untuned sits this king and his
    hand is on the sword

FOOTNOTE TO A POST-LYRICAL POEM

Only there are two birds
wingbeat and wingbeat
half-way, half-way
over this sky
and when the poem is used up
(don't mistake me: I give it you
in reason and not otherwise)
I don't know why
these remain   winging   so very tired

NOW LET'S SOCK IT TO THE SCHOOLS

He made a pass at the love poem.
It married money and stared
back at him from racecourses and 1001 first nights.

He returned to Nature
but even the wildebeest sprang to attention

whimpering *baas,* while in the distance
some raucous birds spread the word.

He laid hold of history
with pentameter and plumb-line.
the facts wouldn't level, showing their undersides.

He settled for the sordid present,
his mirror backed with flaming prophecies.
He managed a glimpse of the Beast just once, one morning while
   shaving.

So he rose to protest
failing to hear himself in the stamping encores.

One afternoon he finds himself
captive to schoolchildren, thinking how
hard to destruct are the mediums of instruction,
especially the oldest.

SONNET ANNOUNCING THE BIRTH OF THE SOUTH AFRICAN REPUBLIC OF LETTERS

Now that funds have become available
A National Sonnet Centre is planned.
Many works hitherto unsaleable
Abroad are, under the N.S.C. brand,

Guaranteed consumable here at home.
When production at the Centre begins
sufficient quantities of aerial foam,
Proxysyntax and bilexicomins

Will resource the process for many years.
Operatives will reserve their muses, masks
And magic arts, plus roots, familiar tears
and all devotions that the goddess asks.

The National Sonnet Centre extends
A special welcome to its ethnic friends.

Faces, Masks, Animae

WALTER SAUNDERS

Walter Saunders was born in Durban in 1930.

Joint founder and editor, with
Peter Horn, of *Ophir* poetry magazine.

CONTENTS

These poems have appeared in *Unisa English Studies, New Coin, Workshop 6, New Nation, Ophir* and *Front*.

TERRORIST

With one eye closed I turn off half the world,
I turn it off and turn it on again,
being a god and all gods having the power
supposing
        (Dammit, ants!)
supposing
        What's that?
           Dragonfly. They stop
dead still in the air and look at you then zip
away like helicopters or flying saucers
faster than the speed of
        What's he think
of me creating a disturbance in his dam
and lying here roasting in the sun
as big as Gulliver's Travels? He knows he can't
do anything about it, I'm the god
around here and I say to him 'Listen,
by shutting one eye I can take away
half your sun. I can take it *all* away. Look,
two eyes. Eclipse!'
        Supposing I'd been there
in those trees, a god, if I'd been there to turn
off the sun, I'd have stopped it
        That sound
pom-pom-pom-pom-pom like the pump starting.
Mother made that terrible cry and rushed in.
They were shouting Stop. And when Mr Ferrio helped
her out, I thought she couldn't walk, I thought
it had happened to her, too.
        'Take the child away,
why didn't someone take the child away?'

Stupid Mrs Banner tried to tell me
a picture had fallen from the wall but
I knew because Colonel Fraser said to father
that day 'The study's a dangerous place,
you're a sitting duck in the study, Charles.'

The army trucks began to arrive.
        They were
putting on my grey suit and I was crying,

a big tear splashed on my new shiny shoes.
I can see it: a big tear on those shiny shoes.

We went in Aunt Ru's car through the plantations,
it was getting dark
            but I'd have made
it dark long before, I'd have made
it dark just as they aimed, I'd have.

AT WOPKO'S PRIVATE EXHIBITION

faces look in from another world

        tania scented the air like a greyhound
                (all that carnaby gear)
        quincey popped out of corners:
                'what does it mean?
                what does it say?
                surely it must say something?'
black lightning
drums   'I want to buy *you*'
                                'what will you pay?'
                                '15 cents,
                                15 cents to hang you on
                                        the wall!'
SLAVES FOR SALE
        nick and tania played noughts and crosses
        in tania's fishnet stockings
                (nick's tiddly laugh)

        in the pantry she opened her mouth wide
        and gave him a kiss like cobweb

cannibal eyes

                                'that is a christ head'
                                'that's like a christ'
                                'yes, I've bought that'

baluba
baule
benin

                    'of course his wife's jealous'
                    'nick's such an ass'
                    'what's he sulking for?'

propitiate
propitiate

VRYSTAAT!
No-one interferes with us;
we play with ourselves.

Vortzog puts the ball into the scrum
and Vortzog heels against the head
and Vortzog picks it up and runs right
into the blindside.

          He's down.
          He's up again.
          No, he's down.
Yes, there's no doubt this time he's taking
the tight-head count and if I'm not mistaken
his right cheek is ornamented with a trickle
of red blood corpuscles.

At last referee Prof. Vortzog has blown his whistle
and awarded a penalty where the scrimmage took place.

Now he's talking to both sets of Vortzogs.
They all shake hands.

The crowd is silent.
Vortzog kicks the ball

          up
          up
          up

It's a tremendous kick.
It's still going up.
The army helicopter quickly moves out of the way.
And still the ball is going up.
It isn't out yet.

The crowd is cheering,
pandemonium is about to break loose.
The police link arms.
The photographers are taking photographs.
and still it's going up   up   up

Now it seems to have burst.
Yes, it *has* burst.

Good Lord, it's full of streamers,
                gas masks.
                tape recorders.

What a *tour de force!*

The spectators are still looking up,
there seems to be something else;
Can you make it out, Chick?

                "All I can see are black clouds coming up."

Chick is busy with the field-glasses.

                "Wait a minute, as a matter of fact
                there *is* something over to the right.
                It looks like FOUR HORSEMEN!"

Four Horsemen?

                "It must be some kind of trick."

Do you think the, the Deity would play a trick?

                "Well, not exactly, Charles."

He certainy would *not*, Chick.

No, I don't think there can be any doubt
about it:

                Divine Revelation!
Yes, there's the Trump,
                the Trump!

What a simply glorious afternoon!

And now great letters are appearing in the sky.
No, I don't need the glasses, thank you, Chick,
I can read 'em:

PURITY

NATIONHOOD

STATELY PLEASURE DOME
(sounds for electronic voices)

1. PRELUDE & FUGUE
Chorus of feathers: Putta-putta
                           Putta-putta
Glassdoor: Motorboats sleep
Chorus of feathers: Putta-putta
                           S L E E P
(SOUND OF BICYCLES ESCAPING)

2. SALLY SWINGS
Glassdoor: Moustachios like ripe figs
                           Chocolate candelabrums
                           Rooms of deserted people

Chorus of Tenderloin
   Obnubilations: Jumping on to the plank
                                     the plank
                                     the plank
                           s w i n g s

Sally Glassdoor: O my waste
                           My burning dragons
                           I have heliotrope in my
                           I have
                                     Have I
                                     Have I
                                     Have
                           I have butter fingers
                           Look at my knees all sweet and sour

Chorus of Tenderloin
  Obnubilations: She has!
                                      She has!
Sir Stutterheim: Do you remember how we laughed
                               at the museum?
Lady Stutterheim: Marinaded laughter for days!
Sir Stutterheim: Anticlockwise!
Lady Stutterheim: Miracles, too?

(SOUND OF CATATONIC COMMITTEES AND TOMATO CLOCKS)

3. QUINTET FOR WATER BISCUITS
Sally: Blue Peter!
Glassdoor: Ice-cream canoes!
                               Snags in the sky!

Chorus of Feathers: Dabchicks
                                                                         Dabchicks

Glassdoor: In Sal Volatile!
Sally: O my holy innocence!
Chorus of Feathers: Dabbadabba
Sally (sings):   I love you
Chorus of Heavy-balled Grumpers: *Three* on a plank!
Sally: I love you
Chorus of Feathers: ant   ant
                                                         ʇuɐ

(SOUND OF THE FOREPLAY OF TOOTHPICKS)

4. MOONSPONGE SWAREE
Sir & Lady Stutterheim: balla balla
                                           balla BALLOOO

Sally: I like juniper
Sir & Lady Stutterheim: balla balla
                                         balla BALLOOO

Sally: Djinn
                               Djinn
Chorus Chororum: S M A S H ! ! !
Glassdoor: No, pianissimo
Chorus Chororum: S M A S H ! ! !
Glassdoor: PIANISSIMO ! ! !
Chorus Chororum: (ppp)   smash
                               (fff)   S M A S H ! ! !

(SOUND OF UN-SOUND)

MEPHISTO

Mephisto: In the overhanging Blue Pavilion,
glass-domed,
         the aging Doctor sits
among the honoured guests.

A wedding feast:
Mr Menelassos is called from his bride
to an urgent consultation
on steel.

CARNIVAL! ! !

Up the escalator
a wolf
a cat
a priest
a goat
an ass:

huge heads weave among the guests

On the cabaret stage,
his voice insinuating
from the pod of a cerise fold,
Paris plays the accordion
to the bride's loquacious smile:

You Are So Beautiful.

The doctor watches,
eyes mist –

trapdoor to the brain,

a whiff!

and I make my entrance
in locust headpiece and suit:

        I have brought the deed.

exaggerate the bow,
watch him, that trembling fist.

Faustus: *Fetch fire to warm this blood.*

Mephisto: No heart within the carapace,
no organs, lights,
                    only sounds
and in this insect dome
mirrors to enlarge his pain:

Give me your arm.

Fierce blood ripples, shines,
fire seals the bond.
What does he call for?
Knowledge? Power? Love?
He will call it love,
assume the accordion player's shape,
employ my charms.

Skyros:
the pleasure yacht
riding at bay:

Faustus: *When we've finished eating*
                    shall we go to bed?

Helen: *Oh, lover, that's the nicest thing*
                    I ever heard you say!

Mephisto: Walpurgis Night!

He rides whirlwinds
to her mountain lair,

sees, hot within her gaze,
wolf   cat   priest   goat   ass.

Well, a devil doesn't pare his nails.

I shift scene,
set the mob smashing his retorts,
watch his laboratory swim.

Chymic haze!

I change shape, time,
become buttonhole raconteur,
know nothing of the Doctor;

I tell them about a dive in the Aegean,
sailors hurling wine-cups against   the walls,
and this blonde doll pulling me down under the table,
husking

CHILD AND DOLL

> "my doll is wearing an evening dress
> and fur coat

> I can change her hair too

> she can have a pony
> or half a pony
>   or plaits"

in a corner
by the fireplace

a large sheet of glass before her

> *through the glass*
> *darkness coming in*

her saucer eyes intense
knitted close together
and beside her for the unlit fire
pine cones and fine pine needles

SON

1. MORNING
goes up to the wall
takes a moth

I say, 'Go and frighten your mother'

she says, holding her throat
'I don't want to see'

and afterwards at the foot of the bed
he says, 'Alright, moth, now you can fly away'

    2. AFTERNOON
        'Are all the soldiers buried here?'
        'No, this is just so people can remember
        them'

in the Magaliesberg foothills
a diminutive chapel, granite, squat

        'Where are they buried?'

dead names

Sidi Rezegh, Alamein, Cassino
lawns cropped smooth like a bullet head
spiked aloes, a lily pond

    g l o r i o s a

        'TADPOLES
        TADPOLES'

        'Quiet, you must be quiet, children'

granddad (R.S.M., now whitehair) says, 'They
ring a bell. The two, standing at ease, come
to attention.'

        'Come and look at the tadpoles
        come and look at the tadpoles'

        he didn't want to go inside because
        he'd seen it at the Klapperkop Museum:

        the dead general in a chair

the soldier outside a tent
with his leg chopped off

'And at exactly 9.30 the light falls on the book'
            ''WE DIED AT SUCH A PLACE . . . .''

                              3. NIGHT
                              she tucks him up, 'You
                              mustn't come into our
                              bed tonight'

                              'Oh dear, just when I *know*
                              I'm going to have a nightmare'

                              'How do you know?'

                              'After that *chapel*?'

DIANA
O spare me, circling hounds;
Have I not fed you with my own hands?

'don't fall down the steps
and thank you very much
for the beautiful flowers'

                              the previous summer
                              a sculptor climbed with her
                              to the mountain top
                              (they had set out as agreed
                              from the cypress trees
                              by the cemetery gate)

                              he had the thunder-caster's beard
                              eyes like saddle leather
                              rock-to-beat sledge-hammer arms

                              they met at a congress on Cycladic
                              art (she wondered how long they
                              would sit watching one another
                              through menagerie glass)

                              to the roof of the world

you see the whole island
the sea many many miles
even the mainland when it is clear
there is an old church
we can sleep there'

'that was a butterfly flick
but it wasn't in the right place
I got that from Myrrhine's sexbook
there's also an icecream whirl
you must go you must go'

'in the dark ages
they would have burnt you
as a witch'

'but my spirit would have lasted'

'they would have burnt you
over and over again'

he crouched by a wall
wrenched a plant free
'smell!'
                    'mm, thyme!'

she remembered
wild hyacinths
a goat on a rock
an old woman with
two hens in a basket

she felt the leopard
spring in his tread
saw when he helped her
the fur
on the back of his hands

nearing the top
the wind cut like a knife
it was dusk
the ends of the world were lit
'you will see' he said
'tomorrow it will be even better'

orange petals
on a blue ground

her room
an aquarelle by Nolde

'Last week
I did a strange thing
I wrote to a Rumanian
I was trying my fate'

greedily they went down
in the bones of the church
teeth upon lips and neck
her breasts wrenched by hands
still smelling of thyme

under the faded
no longer eyes
of ecstatic saints
her body shoved
rocked
deliciously rammed

he thought
'how Damiens died'
into whose open flesh
they poured metal
while the crowd gorped

the next day
the long descent
he went first
(fire out of his eyes)
yes, he wanted to
hurry away
now
the island?
it was enough
he thought of his studio
commissions
only aware of her
when she stumbled

it was like working on a block
challenging the demon
to come out and be mastered
then turning away from it
they could throw it down
the mountainside for all he cared

                                        he thought of the rubble
                                        at the foot of the Acropolis:
                                        horses, kouroi

'scratch my back
hard hard
ahh, YES
and my hips'

hands circle
cupping her breasts

'it's nice but
I'm not sexy
I feel nothing!'

her breasts dazzle
like moons

                                        at last the cypresses came into view
                                        he heard, was it the wind?
                                        her whimpering

                                        what could he explain?
                                        she was strong
                                        she would learn

                                        but when he looked round
                                        her stoneblue eyes said nothing

                                        one should not look round

'don't fall down the steps
and thank you very much
for the beautiful flowers'

past the swimming-pool
shaped like a coffin
down the grass slope
bursting through the mimosa
thicket he was turned
in a moment into a stag

PRELLER '72
(taken from his exhibition at the Pretoria Art Museum)

a man wearing the mask
of a Babylonian magus
(beard thick honeycomb)
hides an empty beertin
behind a tree, having tried
to drown it in greenwater where
the eyes of goldfish and small
children intimidated him

while
at the plateglass door
a father bends

father with a moustache
and one eye raised:

it's siamese
it must belong to
someone, I think
you'd better put
it down

kitten clasped
neck and cheek

turquoise eyes

he made that colour
himself you don't get
that colour in a tube

Solomon & Sheba
Ellen's Watusi
mythic Africa
faces masks
animae

If you spend enough time with them
they become your friends
and you can talk to them . . .

sometimes it happens by chance . . .

El Greco at the Louvre . . .
old witch, grubby

her skirt held together
with safety pins
she was copying this El Greco
firm sweeping movements
one line embracing a complexity
of muscular curves
and one completely simple
and I understood:
two lines talking to one another

> profile of
> Guna 1970
> a touch of
> Piero ('on my
> way to the Uffizi')

> a small circle (lapis)
> on the neck and from the light-
> gold head a spearpoint
> upwards

> signifying
> stillness
> the unborn son

outside
fountain jets
splashing on stone
daddy, remember when
Judith fell in sopping wet?

a couple on the grass
she leaning on her arm
he sitting rocking forward
arms around knees

near them a child
bouncing on a large
red rubber ball

> *and he said 'those eggs what*
> *do they mean?'*

> *well what do they mean?*

> *they are forms*

> *forms well yes but I can't believe*
> *that forms don't mean something*

his own image
walking in the garden

pieces of silver
pierced flesh
A GREEN APPLE
a man with an astrolabe
Icarus

'This morning on my way to the Uffizi
. . . flowers for the Marchesa . . .
ordered 3 gardenias . . . then walked on
to the Piazza della Signoria . . . people
about everywhere . . . A Sunday morning
parade . . .

'In the middle of the square was a
large fat man in a vest, holding
a cat on a leash . . .

'If I tell you that it was a Siamese
cat, you will imagine my delight . . .
A Siamese with a Squint, a Kink
in its tail, wearing bells & a red
bow, and sitting quite unperturbed
by the traffic & pedestrians . . .
sitting, let me tell you, two paces
from the place where Fra Girolamo
Savonarola was burnt at the stake . . .'
(letter to his sister
Minnie, 1953

in a glass case with

carved crocodile &
head rest

animistic Barotse pot

bronze figurines, Dakar

Masai carving

Malay sandal

mother of pearl shell
from Mahè

faience
boy Horus

my dead child
500-1000 B.C.

bought in Cairo
as a talisman
family picnic 1914
father with a moustache
and one eye raised

aged 5 with older
brother, Maurice
(in sailor suit)

he looks like that
the eyes are the same
cheeks aren't so chubby
but the eyes are the same

he's something of a recluse
isn't he?

his own image
half in shadow
a ghost
smoking a
cigarette
magian

in his room
at Dombeya

6 candelabra
5 the branch of a tree
4 books on the floor
3 calabash pots
2 chairs
1 bed

ANASTASIA

1
to Delphi

luxury road
luxury bus
looking down
on the brown tracks
deep in the valley
'the place where three roads meet'
while the guide
blackmaned, Adonic
droned on
in ponderous
execrable English

Nik tried to shut his ears
tried to see the world through glass
saw mainly his fellow pilgrims
cameras, opaque glasses, gewgaws

> *as ye came from the holy land*

separation
blindness

> *met you not my true love*
> *by the way you came?*

separation
makes a eunuch

> To Eloise the Abbot of Cluny
> had written:
>
> "you will be re-united
> where beyond these voices
> there is peace"

Parnassus half-
hidden in cloud
'they are liquidating the wolves by shooting,
at Arakhova they will purchase you wolfskins'

patches of snowfleece
by the roadside

to sleep in a blanket of snow!

and he remembered when
Anastasia had said
'I want to make love
forever'

2
and he remembered saying to her
'the last thing she saw
before she lost consciousness
was the pattern on the wallpaper'

'who?'

'your namesake, the Tsar's daughter,
at Ekaterinburg
after the shooting the soldiers
went round bayoneting
clubbing with rifle butts
to make sure they were dead
one of them bashed her jaw
that's why she had difficulty
with identification later'

'but what nonsense, no-one escaped'

'*she* did – when they were
taking the bodies out to the trucks
one of the soldiers heard her groan
and hid her

the reds denied all rumours
put out a top-level alert

and the whites brought up
a special ambulance train

but the soldier and some others
took her west in a cart

without her "beloved ones"
all she wished to do was die'

3
It had begun three years before
with *The General Line*
in the Embassy lounge
all those plush chairs
shunted forward to meet it

and afterwards
glasses ranged
on silver trays

Nik stood apart from his friends
gulping whiskey
('the sword hangs over us all')
when he became aware of a voice
like a voice in the dark on a ship's deck
typhoon direct ahead
and corposants

'it's all very well
to go to the circus
and *see* someone eat fire
but it's another thing
to do it yourself'

she smiled
her face transfigured
Hogarth's shrimp girl

no, no
when you *see*
it is different

no chance identification

4
a week later they sat
on her Shiraz carpet
with a flask of wine,
salad, chicken,
while the sun poured
through and the shadows
of the branches made
patterns: touch
merge break apart
touch merge

5
'things are slipping away
why? why? why?
"don't panic Anastasia
you mustn't panic"
that's why I cry –

because it can't be
permanent
because I know it's
hopeless, silly
I felt it the other day
when I cried remember?
I thought I'd got over that
and now I feel it over again
d'you know what I mean?
you don't, you don't
it's a feeling just here
you don't know
you're not in love with me
you don't feel it at all'

6
one night they had slept, woken, made love

she was in the bath
he wandering round the bedroom
head still swimming with wine
then he opened the door
onto the bathroom glare

her back to him
the charm and strength
of a Degas

he put a foot in the water
and she said:

'no, no, I've never bathed
with anyone in my *life*
I'm saving that for my husband'

7
Nik under a pergola over a bottle of wine

'*they*'ve got too much hold on you
when you're married – wife, children too
so I told her I was already married
it was a bond of impermanence between us

and there was this other chap, Basil,
an archaeologist, a real expert,
who could draw the magic
out of any piece of pottery you showed him

and who used to talk about th need to "work"
at improving things:
human relationships, society, politics –
it sounds tame
but when the caterpillars are devouring
every green leaf
it's enough to get your name on the secret files

then one day as I was on my way out
she said:
       "leave it a fortnight, sweetie,
       it's very nice, I'm very fond
       of you but you impede me
       you do, you really do
       I can't deepen my attachment
       to Basil when you're around" '

8
on the day Nik agreed
to stop seeing her
they had lunch
at the Semiramis

'next time we must go
to The Crazy Horse'

'Anastasia, what
are you saying?'

9
when her presence
and his rhetoric
no longer protected him from the abyss
he thought of his friends
in the resistance

thought of the misery
below the surface on the streets:
men leaving home at 4 in the morning
to work for half a wage
returning at 9 or 10 at night

thought of Father G – –
on trial before the military court:
false charges
perjured evidence

the state press
spreading compost on the lie

and he thought of
caterpillars

10
Alexander J. Sewer behind his desk

'they're one hundred per cent on our side
the real law and order guys
and it's dangerous too
they get threats
and some pretty ugly things happen to their families
of course it's got its compensations
they're on double pay
with a bonus for every name they screw
but what I like about them
well patriotism's not enough
it's the right attitude to the job
you know: "don't ask us to pull a cart
or eat dried oats
but if it's man's work we'll do it." '

> *Nik under a pergola etc.*
>
> 'I was tipped-off by a friend
> in the Foreign Affairs Department
> so I crossed the border that night.
> Anastasia? it had been over
> between us for some time
> she was about to marry Basil
> she knew nothing, nothing
> I never thought for a moment
> the bastards would pick her up'

11
'look at these nice boobs
like grapefruits
hey dolly you like
your guy to grab them like this?
why don't you tell us
where he is?'

'what they need is some
beauty treatment'

'scientific'

'here give us that cigar'

in a room on the terrace
surrounded by flats
(washing, aerials
blank faces at the windows)
her screams were drowned
by a motorbike engine
and a cauldron
beaten like a gong
fingers thrust up
her vagina, twisted
face devil-eyed
against hers: 'sing
communist bitch sing!'
        at A – – –,
        B – – – – Street,
        while on the sunny heights
        pilgrims
        whose world was being made safe
        clicked cameras at the columns